Haley Sharon creates stickers
under the name "MadebyHayHay"

Adam Strohschein makes music
under the name "Quasar Kelly"

QUASAR KELLY

Check out other books from **"Gently
Insert This Into Your Life Publishing"**

Book Cover Design by: Haley Sharon

Illustrations by: Haley Sharon

First Edition 2025

ISBN: **979-8-218-65926-4 (Paperback)**

Library of Congress Control Number: 2025907254

DON'T BE A BITCH

(A book of advice and wisdom
with cute illustrations)

Written By:
Adam Strohschein
Haley Sharon

Illustrations By:
Haley Sharon

This book has a playlist
included to act as a
soundtrack, the music was
picked out from the authors.
Just scan the QR code and
enjoy!

Don't be a b**ch

Don't be a bitch

If you give up on something, it means you didn't want it badly enough. No matter how many barriers you may encounter, and you still hold onto the fact you will obtain it means you already have it.

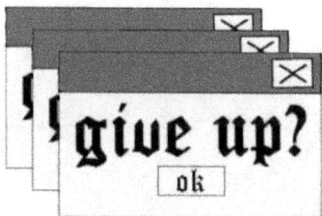

Your brain can create some
of the greatest scenarios,
don't take it as fact.
It's just thoughts and
thoughts can change.

Go drink some water and
stop being a bitch.

Don't be a b**ch

Don't shit on someone else's dreams, those are their dreams, not yours. Just as someone could do the same to you.

Once you don't give someone what they want, that's when you truly see them.

Be patient with people, they
may be going through shit
that they don't talk about.

If they wanted to they would.

Don't be a b**ch

Not everyone has the same
love language as you.
Understand they don't care
any less for you, they just
have a different way of
showing it.

The only person you can rely
on for happiness is yourself.
Once you place that on
someone else they
determine when you are.

Don't be a b**ch

Seriously, go drink some
water
...bitch

Take a moment and look
around you.

This won't last forever

let me say that again

this
<u>won't</u>
last
forever.

Don't be a b**ch

Some people are meant to
leave your life, they simply
are there to teach you a life
lesson and move on.

Just let them <u>go,</u>
it's time to move on.

Keep people in your life that
support your wins.

Keep people in your life that
not only support the wins

but also <u>support you</u>

when you fail.

Don't be a b**ch

Do you ever find yourself looking back at the things you went through and think.

"Those problems were nothing compared to what I'm going through now" ...

Your future self is saying that about whatever you're going through right now.

Your mind gives up before
your body does, push
yourself.

Don't be a b**ch

Always know your self-worth
and <u>never</u> settle for anything
less.

Don't act like a dollar bill

when you know you're a
fucking diamond.

All the shitty things that
happen are just character
development and story arc in
the tv show of your life.

When someone is telling you
a story,

listen to them.

They are taking the time to
open up to you and deserve
your undivided attention.

When you're wrong about something, admit it.
We are all human and make mistakes.
Taking responsibility and the initiative to learn from it is a respective quality.

P.S. Don't be a bitch about it either.

Don't be a b**ch

If you ever feel like you didn't
accomplish anything today,
just remember...

you got out of bed...

little steps are still steps.

When you least suspect it...

that's when good things
happen.

Don't be a b**ch

Once you place boundaries in your life that's when you weed out the fake.

A true person who is meant to be there won't make you feel bad about it.

It's cost $0 to be an asshole,

it also costs $0 to be nice.

Don't be a b**ch

Jobs don't care about you,

they can replace you,

just as you replaced someone,

you know what can't be replaced?

Time.

Time spent with your friends,
time spent with your family,
time spent with your kids,
time spent with your pets,
time spent with yourself.

Spend time with them.

Not your job.

Adam Strohschein & Haley Sharon

Whatever you're going through in life, someone holds the answers to your questions.

Most times,

its you,

listen.

Don't be a b**ch

It's funny...

When we are young we try
so hard to grow up fast.

When we get older we try so
hard to be young again.

However,

you can always revisit your
inner child, do something
today your younger self
would have wanted to do.

Give someone you know a
random gift.

Doesn't have to be big.

Go thrifting,
find something of yours,
doesn't matter how big or
small it is, as long as it comes
from the heart and shows
you were thinking of them.

Don't be a b**ch

Right now,
Take a deep breath,
Hold it for 3 seconds.

1... **2**.. **3**...

Exhale,

relax.

Now, go kick ass today.

If you ever feel insecure
about someone's past...
just remember,
you have a past too.

Different people make
different memories.

Don't be a b**ch

Do you ever find yourself
having a bunch of tasks to
accomplish on a day off and
not doing any of them?

Don't be pissed at yourself,

sometimes you need a day
to relax and recharge.

You may think you have
control of your life, but you
don't.

You can try with all your
power to control situations,
people,
events,
outcomes, etc.

You do have the power to
make choices,

choices that determine your
outcome

be wise with your choices.

Don't be a b**ch

If you want someone in your
life to change
ask yourself

*"What did you like about this
person when you first met
them"*

People only change when
they want to

if it's not a genuine change

they haven't changed.

When someone close to you
lashes out at you take a
moment and put yourself in
their shoes.

Give them space.

They may be hurting, and they
will come to you when they are
ready,

be patient.

Don't be a b**ch

Let's say you have a goal, but after waiting for so long you start to lose hope it'll happen.

Another opportunity comes along that's not quite like your planned goal,
but it's here now.

Don't settle for second best.

Why settle for a snack

When you can have the main course.

Be the kind of person to lean on, they might need it just as much as you do.

Don't be a b**ch

Take some time to create
your own space, fill where
you live with things that
make you happy. Have it be
an extension of yourself. And
whenever life becomes
stressful or people become
hurtful, simply retreat there
and be surrounded by your
own happiness, it all starts at
home.

When you have multiple projects or tasks, break them down based on importance and do them one at a time. It's easy to become overwhelmed when thinking about all of them at once. So pick one and start, take a break from time to time but stick with it till it's done. Remember to also take a moment once you complete said task and look back on the journey, feel that sense of accomplishment, purpose and worth. Take it all in and then move onto the next project.

Don't be a b**ch

We are constantly being
tested,
every situation,
every person,
every feeling,
is here to test how you will
act/react.
So before you fall back into
old habits, step back.
Relax,
breathe,
feel whatever emotions this
brings to you and decide
how you want to move on,
try a different approach.

Our lives are like a big
scrapbook filled with
moments with people.

Some we don't talk to,
some we do,
some that passed on,
some we lost touch with.

However, they always have a
page in our book.

Don't be a b**ch

You're stronger than you think.

Every mistake you've made
has led you to this moment.

Don't think of it as a bad
thing.

Think of it as your meant to
be here at this moment with
all the knowledge to guide
you.

Don't be a b**ch

If you ever find yourself in a
situation where you want to
cry but not be judged

1. Find yourself a
   graveyard
2. Find yourself a
   random gravestone
3. Cry as much as you
   want

cause no one is going to
think twice as to why you are
crying in a graveyard.

Remember your time and
energy are very important.

Give it to people that deserve
it.

Not to those who drain it and
want more.

Don't be afraid of the unknown,

embrace it,

that's when magical things happen.

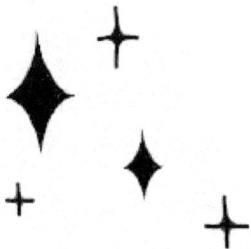

You can do anything for 30 seconds.

Don't be a b**ch

You're not always going to
have the same interests as
other people.

But don't change who you
are to please them.

If they don't like who you are
already they don't deserve to
know you.

Why should you give a fuck about what others think?

Listen to that song you love on repeat.

Watch that tv show people hate but you like.

Go create that art thing you wanted to.

Spend time with that person who you like being around.

Have a dream? Go get it.
Only person stopping you...

is you.

Don't be a b**ch

When we lose old friends or they don't match your current energy it's upsetting, but you must understand it just means you are leveling up to a new era of yourself.

One that will make room for new friends and experiences.

Happy birthday new you!

Good things will come to
you when you are patient,
so calm the fuck down
already ok?
Just enjoy the ride.

Don't be a b**ch

While it's always good to
live in the present, it's also a
good idea to plan.

Future you will thank the
past you.

If you find yourself in a situation looking for answers, try looking at the past you might be surprised by what you find.

Don't be a b**ch

Nobody is entitled to your personal business, so be careful with what you share. Sometimes people lay silent with envy and jealousy waiting for you to fail so they can take joy in it. Also, keep your secrets with those you can fully trust, a snake in the grass will use it as ammunition against you when given the opportunity.

Before starting a new
relationship take time to be
on your own. Rediscover
what brings you joy, work
through your insecurities to
ensure that they won't follow
you to the next one.
You must heal first.

Don't be a b**ch

Sometimes when life becomes too much, you may think about what it's like not to be here anymore. Take a moment in your past when you felt that way and just picture if you were not there anymore from that moment till now. Just think about all the memories and moments you would have missed out on by not being here.

I know sometimes you want to say what's on your mind.

Sometimes it's best to know when to speak and when to be silent, let karma handle the rest.

Don't be a b**ch

Not everyone is going to like you and that's perfectly fine.
Don't focus on those who don't, focus on those who do.

If you keep up with that attitude Santa Claus won't visit you.

Don't be a b**ch

Don't let defeat define who you are, instead learn from it so next time you can win.

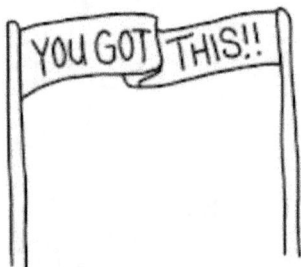

Be and stay humble,
if not, something or
someone will do that for
you.

Don't be a b**ch

Live the life you want as if
you already have it as time
goes on you'll live it.

Take a chance on that
person or thing, you might
be surprised by the results.

Don't be a b**ch

Keep in mind that if someone doesn't treat you the way you want, there is always someone else that will.

You may look up to someone that talks about doing something, but how about you look up to someone that actually does it.

Actions speak louder than words.

Don't be a b**ch

Take yourself out on a date,

show yourself how
amazing you are,

Love starts with you, from
within.

Why are you so hard on
yourself?
Don't you think you've
done enough to cut
yourself down?

If you can't love yourself,
how are you supposed to
love someone else?

Don't be a b**ch

Sometimes when someone comes to you with a problem, they don't want you to tell them what they did wrong or should have done.

They may just want a person to listen to them without judgment.

It's not always about you.

Society has taught us that
crying is a sign of
weakness.
That's complete bullshit.

Go ahead and cry!

Feel any emotion that
comes to you.

Be a human!

Not a robot.

77

Don't be a b**ch

People will hurt you, even if they promise not to. No one is perfect and believing they are is very foolish. We all make mistakes.

When giving someone advice, it come from the heart, from your personal experiences. Tell them what you learned and how you handled it. What they choose to do with that information is on them. But remember in a world full of people that only want to hear what makes them feel good, be real and be honest. If they don't like it guaranteed later on they will be thanking you.

Don't be a b**ch

Just because you don't see results right away doesn't mean it's not working. Keep doing it till it's a habit, till it's a part of your everyday life. Then look back on the moment you first started, you'll be surprised.

Repitition is Key

Always focus on yourself and
when you feel you've
reached your goal create
another to achieve.
Keep going,
never stop,
and always remember you
can do it if you want to bad
enough.

Don't be a b**ch

Every single day you can make money, what do you like to do? Research ways to make money from it. Starting off you may not be able to quit your day job. So start it off as a hobby, something you do in your free time. Then expand it once you become confident into a side hustle. From there if you become financially stable from it turn that into your job. You need to have confidence in whatever you do and most importantly in yourself. Once you have that <u>nothing</u> can stop you.

Never let a person push
you around or make you do
anything you don't want to
do. Be vocal about it and
let them know they won't
treat you like that, let no
one mistreat you ever.

Don't be a b**ch

Don't wait around for people to do things with you, if they want to they will and if no go on your own and enjoy. Make your own fun, all you need is yourself.

If you do things in your life with the focus to show off how amazing your life is it looks desperate, it's not cute. Don't go on adventures just for it to be a photo opp to make someone jealous. Live in the moment, take pictures for yourself to enjoy for later on, this isn't a popularity contest high school is over.

Don't be a b**ch

The way you treat people is often a reflection of how you view yourself.

While remembering the past
may be nostalgic, it also can
lead back to bad feelings.
While it's exciting to think of
the future it can be
exhausting wondering how
you'll get there.
Live in the present,
the past is over.
The future isn't here yet so
you can create the one you
want right now.

Don't be a bch**

It won't create itself.

The people that hurt us the
deepest are those we love
and care about the most.

Don't be a b**ch

A heartfelt apology is one of
the toughest things to do.

However, it's always the right
thing to do.

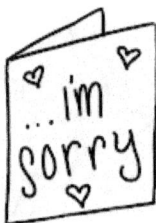

In your darkest moments
those who stood by your side
will never be forgotten.

Don't be a b**ch

Always trust the voice inside you.

If something doesn't feel right,

don't do it.

Being rejected is just
someone's way of showing
that they couldn't see the
potential you have.

Show them what they lost
out on.

Being in love is one of the
scariest things you
can do.

However, hiding your
feelings and never
expressing them is even
scarier.

If you ever find yourself
being overrun by thoughts.

Spend time in nature,

listen to what it has to say.

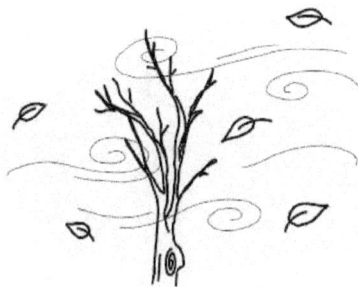

Don't be a b**ch

You can never return to the past.

So why let it control your future decisions?

As much as we sometimes
enjoy the company of people

the one person you should
<u>always</u> enjoy is yourself.

Don't be a b**ch

Prove them wrong.

Whenever you can't find
the words to
express yourself,

let music do it for you.

Don't be a b**ch

Surround yourself with
people who are:
-Strong
-Stable
-Dependable
-Caring
-Kind
-Understanding
-Supportive

they should be a reflection
of yourself, who you strive
to be.

If you ever feel like you aren't cool enough, just keep in mind you have a fan out there watching you from the crowd, someone who wishes they could be you.

Don't be a b**ch

Whenever we go through a breakup it's always easy to say what was wrong on their end.

Put your ego aside and ask yourself;

"What can I do to make my next relationship better?",

"How can I avoid the same mistakes?"

Learn from your mistakes, don't keep repeating them.

Did you drink that water
yet?

Put this book down and
get some, and don't give
the whole "I don't like
water it doesn't have a
taste" of course it doesn't...
it's water. Go put some of
that flavoring in it and stop
making excuses. You
seriously think you can live
off energy drinks and
lattes?

Don't be a b**ch

When we do things for
people it can fill their cup
up when it's empty.

but the more you give
someone..

Don't be a b**ch

the less you have...

until you don't have any...

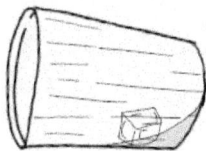

Don't be a b**ch

Remember to keep your
cup filled at the same time.

Do what makes you happy.

Don't be a b**ch

Remember when things
get tough and you wish
they would "go back to
normal" they can't.

That's the old life you had;
you're becoming stronger
as time goes on.

If you start something new today it just might be the thing to change your life.

Don't be a b**ch

Once you break someone's trust you never get that back. So always be mindful of your words and actions. Even if you break it and they tell you they trust you still, deep down inside they don't. It's easier to hide the pain and pull back than let those walls down to get hurt again.

You never truly know a
person till you see them at
their worst. When all that
ego and pride gets
knocked down and they
become vulnerable. That's
when you catch a glimpse
at their hidden self, the one
they lock away.

Don't be a b**ch

Spend time getting to know your parents, grandparents, siblings, or friends on a deeper level. Ask them questions you may not normally ask. Ones that may seem embarrassing to you. They won't be around forever, and their answers may give you a new sense of respect or outlook that you may never have known about them. Anything you've gone through more than likely they have as well and it's comforting knowing those close to you have experienced what you have.

Holding onto anger from how someone did you wrong can lead to bitterness that can flow into a new friendship or relationship. That's not fair to them or yourself. Forgiveness may not be easy or necessary for another person that did something to hurt you, forgive yourself and understand that you didn't deserve that hurt. Don't hold onto it and carry it around.

Don't be a b**ch

Take pride in how you present yourself, while you shouldn't care what other people think making a first impression is always a lasting memory people will have of you, so make it a good memorable one.

Always be your true
authentic self, alot of
people become what they
think people want them to
be and in turn do and say
things they never would in
order to impress or fit in.

Don't be a b**ch

You have lessons to learn, if you ignore them you'll continue to experience them till you do.

Whenever you find yourself
discontent with your current
life remember a time when
you had joy or felt happiness.
Take yourself back to those
moments, what was going
on? Who was there?

If you ever want to be there
just simply close your eyes
and remember.
You'll be there.

Don't be a b**ch

Next time you have a few
moments to spare while out
and about, just sit in your
vehicle with the windows
down and just observe the
world around you.
Listen to the atmosphere,
feel the wind, smell the air,
just be in the moment.

You should always strive to better yourself.

To become stronger mentally and psychically.

Every single day.

Don't be a b**ch

Remember not everyone is perfect, you can pick apart anyone in your life to justify what <u>you</u> feel is perfect, however we are all flawed and will never be perfect.

Listen to your favorite song
and read the lyrics.

What about it really sticks
with you?

Spend time with people that
match your energy.

You might be the bad guy
in someone's story,
you are also the good guy
in someone else's.

It's all about perspective.

perspective

Don't be a b**ch

You've been through many
things before this and you'll
be through many more
things.
But, we need you.
You may not understand
yet, one day everything will
make sense.
Just hold on and try again
tomorrow.

It always gets better,
sometimes it may not
seem so.

You need rest,
just relax and take
everything in.

Don't be a b**ch

You have people in your life
that want you to win.

Don't let them down.

Think about this,
what if it worked out?
If everything you ever
imagined unfolded before
you.
Don't stop now.

Don't be a b**ch

You have to understand no matter what happens or how many promises are made, people with hurt you. We are all flawed, it's a part of the human experience and what you decide to say or do from that is up to you, act accordingly.

Discipline will get you further than motivation.

Do what needs to be done, even if you don't feel like it.

Don't be a b**ch

You may not feel that you've been successful in your life, make a list of things in the past five years you've done. At first you may not be able to think of that many things, talk to friends and family, you'll be surprised by what they remember.

Fail at everything you do.

Completely break down your ego and from there keep failing till you can't anymore. Ever win will have a deeper meaning and you'll appreciate it more.

Don't be a b**ch

If things seem tough when
you start to better yourself,
do not give up. Let that spark
that started the fire in the
first place grow into an out of
control blaze that completely
reduces your old self/life to
ashes and from there rise up
like the phoenix and spread
those wings.

Please keep going, not for
anyone else but yourself.

Whenever you find yourself filled with negative thoughts and feelings, redirect your mind to tasks you have to complete.

Focus on the tasks,

act out the process in your mind, step by step as you plan on doing it.

This helps get your brain out of whatever is bothering you and onto something else more constructive.

Repeat whenever you need to.

Don't be a b**ch

It's nice to have people around you that always think what your working on is amazing, but for a different approach get opinions from those that don't know you. Their perspective won't be on you but what you're presenting and from there you'll get a more honest response.

You can become whoever you want to be.

It's simple,

create an alter ego.

Who is that person?

What do they have in life?

What do they look like?

How do they interact with others?

Ask yourself a series of questions just like this, create this person you'd like to be. Then once in a while do something your alter ego would do, take a different route home, order a different drink, change you're your body language, try a different meal. Simple steps that overtime will transform you into whoever it is you want to be.

Don't be a b**ch

"Don't worry, I'll do it later" is the biggest lie you tell yourself and let me guess usually bites you in the ass right? Do it now or when you have available time. Procrastinating turns you weak overtime, it's easy to push things to the side since "right now" isn't convenient. Well, when whatever was supposed to be done isn't it becomes inconvenient and could have easily been avoided.

Just do the damn thing already

P.S. go drink some water too.

Shitty people always get what they got coming to them, it may take time but in the end they always do.

Get the popcorn ready.

Don't be a b**ch

Anger is natural, what isn't is trying to hide it and when it does come out after being held in for so long is often an outburst that hurts others and yourself. Find an outlet for your anger, in psychical activities, screaming a song in your car, just something that gets your inner built up energy out in a positive way.

You can learn anything you've ever wanted to. All the information is out there, you just have to find it and want the knowledge bad enough.

Don't be a b**ch

You only have so many moments on this earth and sadly can end unexpectedly. We all have dreams that seem out of reach and scary to obtain, what's even scarier is a live unfulfilled, one with the "should of", "could of" of a dream left to fade. You become a powerful force once you put forth effort into chasing a dream, in fact unstoppable.

Self-pity is a dangerous game that we all play from time to time. It's easy to slip into and hard to get out of , to relive every past mistake and slowly drift deeper and deeper until all hope is lost. Thing is, hope is never lost it's simply forgotten. Just remember you can always turn things around with just a little **hope**.

Don't be a b**ch

We all have things we don't want to do in life, yet we have to do them. We can express our dislike for said task, try a different approach. Tell yourself that once you complete it you'll give yourself a treat for doing it. You'll find yourself wanting to get it over with in order to get the reward.

Write a letter to yourself and open it up a year from now. Tell yourself how you are currently feeling, what you are working on, where you want to be, where you want to go.

Talk to yourself directly as if you are writing a long lost friend, then forget the letter until you find it later on. You'll be surprised at how much you've changed in just a year.

Don't be a b**ch

People only feel sorry for you so many times when you make the same mistakes. Listen to their advice, if they are taking the time to point you in the right direction and give you piece of mind, respect what they say and apply it to your situation. You may not like what they say since the truth hurts. Rise above, learn, grow, become stronger.

Fool me once shame on you,

Fool me 20 times, get your shit together and stop fucking up you're making your friends sad and Santa Claus ain't coming this year.

Once a day give thanks for what you have, it's easy to look at what we don't have.

Be grateful you get to live a life, to create, to love, to laugh.

Give thanks for the bad times, the dark moments, the ones that forced you to grow into who you are today.

Give thanks for the future, what you want to do, who you want to be.

Don't be a b**ch

Just because your not
where you want to be,
doesn't mean that the
work you are putting in
isn't going to give you
progress.

"Imagine there is a bank account that credits your account each morning with $86,400. It carries over no balance from day to day. Every evening the bank deletes whatever part of the balance you failed to used during the day. What would you do? Draw out every cent, of course? Each of us has such a bank, it's name is time. Every morning, it credits you 86,400 seconds. Every night it writes off at a lost, whatever of this you failed to invest to a good purpose. It carries over no balance. It allows no over draft. Each day it opens a new account for you. Each night it burns the remains of the day. If you fail to use the day's deposits, the loss is yours. There is no drawing against "tomorrow". You must live in the present on today's deposits. Invest it so as to get from it the utmost in health, happiness, and health. The clock is running. Make the most of today."

— Marc Levy, "<u>If Only It Were True</u>"

Don't be a b**ch

Hi

www.ingramcontent.com/pod-product-compliance
Lightning Source LLC
La Vergne TN
LVHW051739080426
835511LV00018B/3146